LILETTE'S KITCHEN

LILETTE EBRAHIMKHAN

Photography : UYEN LUU
Food styling : BEC DICKINSON
Illustrations : TILLY www.runningforcrayons.co.uk
Contributing editors : KATE BASSETT, MIRANDA SUMMERS-PRITCHARD
Art director and design : CLÉMENCE LERAY

Lilette's Kitchen

Lilette Ebrahimkhan

INTRODUCTION
page 1

GAJAKS
page 3

STARTERS
page 17

MEAT
page 29

FISH
page 41

VEGETARIAN
page 53

SIDES
page 75

SPICES CUPBOARD
page 89

INDEX
page 94

ACKNOWLEDGMENTS
page 97

INTRODUCTION

A recipe book! My mother would have laughed at the very thought of it.

But when my daughter, Tayvanie, turned thirty, the only birthday present she wanted was that I write down all my recipes. It was a terrifying thought – I'd never measured out ingredients and had only learned to cook through trial and error, not from any formal training.

I agreed to give it a go and began to think back to my childhood in Mauritius: the sunshine, mango trees, Sunday church service, playing on the beach, big noisy dinner parties and trips to the local food market in Port Louis. My grandfather – a Southern Indian, named Saravanah "Sam" Moorghen – and his cousins owned a row of shops there and would take me every Saturday morning. I'd drink tea, have chilli cakes – gateaux piments – with bread for breakfast and watch my grandfather selling spices. I memorised the name and smell of each one.

My mother was a wonderful cook and would frequently invite family, friends and neighbours to eat with us. I loved the array of home-cooked curries, fish, rice, chapatis and pickles spread out on the table. But my mother always kept me out of the kitchen. She didn't want me to cook – she wanted me to study.

My parents encouraged me to be ambitious, so at the age of seventeen, I moved to the UK to read law at City University. I funded my education by working in a hotel, sharing a room with five other chambermaids. I still couldn't make ends meet, so I ended up dropping out of my law course and switching to nursing at St Margaret's Hospital in Epping, where I met my late husband Paul, a doctor. When Tayvanie and her brother, Krishnan, were born, I wanted to be able to make fresh, healthy meals for my family, so I finally taught myself how to cook. I went to Southern Indian supermarkets, bought the spices I recognised and started experimenting with the tastes and textures I'd known as a child.

My children have always loved my cooking, and since I remarried in 2003, my husband, Rashid, has also been devouring my dishes. Cooking has become a way of not just providing for my family but of entertaining and delighting friends.

This book has been a labour of love – a birthday present to my daughter and a thank-you gift to all my family for inspiring and supporting me. It's also a tribute to my Mauritian mother, who passed away before my children were born. She couldn't keep me out of the kitchen after all. I wish she could have enjoyed my cooking the way I enjoyed hers.

One little note before you dive in – when instructed to allow dishes to cook, please ensure that the pan or cooking pot is covered with its lid to keep the moisture and delicious aromas in. Enjoy!

GAJAKS

MUTTON OR LAMB ROLLS

Preparation time: 60 minutes. Day-before preparation required.
Cooking time: 60 minutes

Serves 10

For the filling
300g boneless mutton or lamb
300g potatoes

For the mutton/lamb marinade
3 finely diced onions
1tbs minced garlic
1tbs minced ginger
1tsp salt
1tbs garam masala
1tbs coriander seeds
1 bunch chopped coriander leaves

2tbs olive oil
5 ground curry leaves
3tbs curry powder (mild or hot according to taste)
250ml vegetable oil for frying

For the casing
3 spring roll pastry sheets (alternatively, filo pastry works well)
3 beaten eggs
1 box breadcrumbs

* Remove all visible fat from the mutton/lamb and finely dice. If you have a food processor, use the chop setting.
* Put the meat into a non-metallic bowl with the marinade spices. Make sure all the meat is coated with the spices.
* Cover and leave in the fridge overnight to marinate.
* The following day, heat the olive oil in a pan over a medium heat. Add the ground curry leaves and curry powder and stir for a couple of minutes. You want to slightly warm the spices, being careful not to let them burn.
* Add the marinated mutton/lamb, cover and cook for 1 hour on a low heat until tender.
* While the meat is cooking, peel and boil the potatoes. Once they are soft, remove from the heat, drain and mash.
* Put the cooked mutton/lamb and mashed potato into a bowl and stir. Allow to totally cool.
* Slice the spring roll pastry sheets in half.
* Put 2tbs of the filling in the middle of a sheet. Roll the pastry with the filling in the centre and fold both ends. Dip/coat (not soak) all sides of the roll in the beaten eggs then roll in the breadcrumbs.
* Deep fry in vegetable oil on a high heat until golden brown. Place on a plate lined with kitchen roll to remove excess oil.
* Serve with sliced cucumber and tomatoes, sprinkled with chopped coriander leaves

ONION BHAJAS (BHAJI)

Preparation time: 60 minutes
Cooking time: 60 minutes

Serves 6

4 large thinly sliced white onions
6tbs gram flour
1tbs salt
1tbs crushed garlic
1tbs garam masala
½tsp haldi (turmeric) mixed with
10ml hot water
1tsp ground coriander seeds
1tsp jeera powder (ground cumin)
15ml water

250ml vegetable oil for frying

* In a large bowl, mix all the ingredients, apart from the oil, into a dough.
* Take a small amount of the mixture, about the size of a large tomato, and roll it into a ball in the palm of your hand and set aside. Repeat for all the mixture, making sure the rolled balls do not touch one another.
* Select a large frying pan or wok and fry in the oil on a medium heat.
* Fry a few balls at a time for 3-5 minutes until the outside is golden brown. These will look darker once you remove them from the oil.
* Place on a plate lined with kitchen roll to remove excess oil. Serve with the coconut sambal (p.12) and the tomato chutney (p. 83).

I can still smell my mother's homemade onion bhajas and hear the sizzle from her kitchen. We couldn't always afford meat, so these were a delicious and affordable savoury appetiser.

FISH SAMOSAS

Preparation time: 40 minutes
Cooking time: 90 minutes

Makes 30

For the filling
2 medium-sized potatoes
2 tins tuna in oil (any boneless
fish can be used)
2tsp ground garlic
¼tsp garam masala
2tsp vegetable oil for making the
paste
1tsp curry powder (mild or hot
according to taste)
4 chopped curry leaves
2 finely chopped onions
4 chopped coriander leaves
1 chopped chilli
Salt and pepper to taste

250ml vegetable oil for frying

For the casing
10 spring roll pastry sheets (or
filo pastry)

* Peel and boil the potatoes. Add a pinch of salt to the boiling water.
* Fry the fish on a high heat until golden brown and remove from the pan. Place on a plate lined with kitchen roll to remove excess oil. Evenly separate the fish flakes.
* Put the remainder of the filling ingredients, including the potatoes, into the pan. Stir well. Let it simmer for 5 minutes before adding the tuna flakes to the cooked paste, stirring well. Let it cool for 5 minutes.
* Fill the samosas: see the how-to on the following pages.
* If you want to freeze the samosas, it is best to do that now, before frying.
* Use a pan tall enough to deep-fry the samosas with enough oil in it to cover the pieces. The oil must be bubbling before you fry the samosas.
* When golden in colour, remove the samosas from the pan using a large, slotted spoon and dab with paper towel to remove excess oil.

Samosas are a family favourite snack. My sister, Jo, always makes batches of meat fish and vege-
table samosas to share at get-togethers.

HOW TO :
FILL THE SAMOSAS

* Unfold the pastry into single sheets and cut into 3 equal lengths.
* Starting at the top left corner, make a triangle shape and put stuffing inside.
* Use 1tsp plain flour and a small amount of water to make a paste to seal the edges of the pastry.

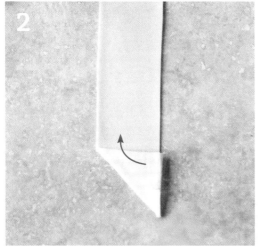

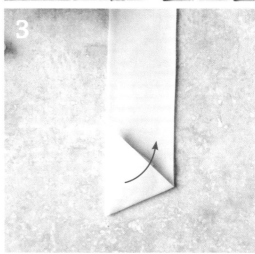

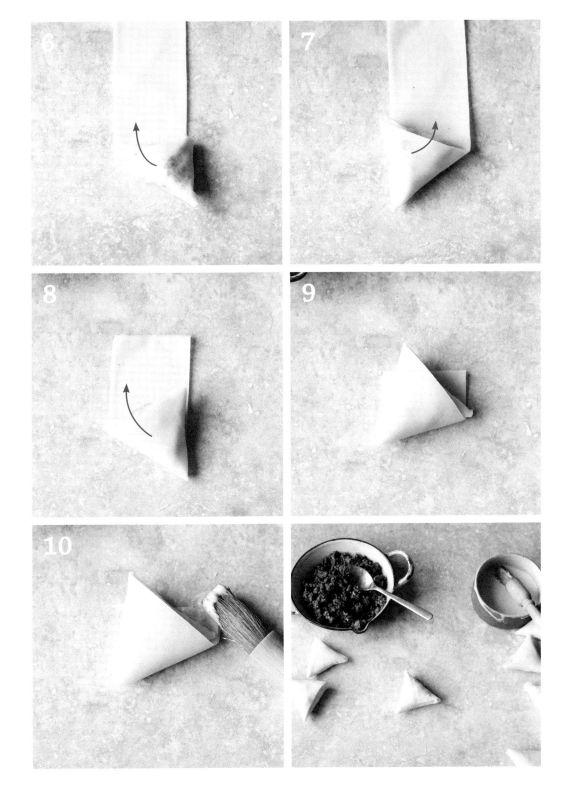

CHILLI CAKES AND COCONUT SAMBAL

Preparation time: 60 minutes. Day-before preparation required.
Cooking time: 90 minutes

Serves 6

For the chilli cakes
200g yellow split peas
1tbs salt
2 finely chopped chillies
10 chopped coriander leaves
2tsp garlic paste
2tsp garam masala

250ml vegetable oil for frying

For the coconut sambal
225g grated coconut
5 dried chillies
2 red onions
1tsp coconut milk
3 fresh mint leaves – removed
from stalk
1tsp tamarind water

* Soak the yellow split peas overnight in water with 1tbs salt.
* For the sambal, mix all the ingredients using a blender. Put in a bowl and allow to chill.
* Remove the soaked yellow split peas and grind using a food processor until soft and grainy.
* In a large bowl, mix the chopped chillies, coriander leaves, garlic paste and garam masala. Stir in the pea mixture and add salt to taste.
* Take a small amount of the mixture, about the size of a tomato, and roll it into a ball in the palm of your hand and set aside. Repeat for all the mixture, making sure the rolled balls do not touch one another.
* Fry around 8 balls at a time until golden brown. Do not overfill your pan, and don't let the balls touch each other.
* Remove from the pan using a large, slotted spoon then place on a plate lined with kitchen roll to remove excess oil.
* Serve hot with the cooled sambal.

Every street stall in Mauritius sells chilli cakes, or gateaux piments. As a child, I'd snack on them every day after school – sometimes stuffing them in bread to make a chilli cake sandwich. Tayvanie, wanted me to make chilli cakes every Sunday for her breakfast and would generously share them with her brother.

AUBERGINE FRITTERS

Preparation time: 30 minutes
Cooking time: 60 minutes

Serves 14

2 large round washed aubergines
300g gram flour
3tsp crushed garlic
3 red or green chopped chillies
1tsp garam masala
1tsp jeera powder (ground cumin)
1 bunch chopped coriander leaves
3tsp salt
1tsp black pepper
4tbs water
250ml vegetable oil for frying

*   Slice the aubergines into thin round slices across the width.
*   Put the slices into a bowl of cold salted water to avoid the aubergine browning.
*   In a large bowl, mix the gram flour, crushed garlic, chopped chillies, garam masala, jeera, coriander, salt, pepper and water.
*   Mix well to a fairly thick paste to create a batter.
*   In small batches of about 4, dip the aubergine slices in the paste and coat evenly.
*   Heat the oil in a deep non-stick pan.
*   Carefully place the coated aubergine in the hot oil and fry until golden brown.
*   Place on a plate lined with kitchen roll to remove excess oil.
*   Repeat the process and serve with the tomato chutney (p. 83).

I used to eat aubergine fritters, or gato brinzel, for breakfast with bread and butter or take them to school in a tiffin box and have them for lunch with my friends. The perfect fritter should be crispy on the outside and soft in the inside.

STARTERS

TANDOORI CHICKEN

Preparation time: 70 minutes. Day-before preparation required.
Cooking time: 60 minutes

Serves 4

1kg chicken breast cut into cubes
2tbs tandoori masala
1 large (400ml) tub plain or coconut yoghurt
1tbs jeera powder (ground cumin)
2tbs crushed garlic
2tbs crushed ginger
1tsp ground black pepper
1tsp salt
¼tsp red chilli powder
spray oil

* Marinate the chicken with all the ingredients and mix well.
* Cover with clingfilm, and marinate in the fridge for at least 1 hour, or overnight if time permits.
* Preheat oven to gas mark 5/180 C.
* Place the chicken on a foil tray and lightly spray with oil, making sure each piece is covered.
* Cover the tray with foil and place in the oven for 30 minutes.
* Remove the foil, turn the chicken and return to the oven for a further 5 minutes to brown both sides.
* Serve with the cucumber and mango salad (p. 78).

Tandoori meat is usually marinated in a spice mix before cooking – typically in a tandoor clay oven or on a charcoal barbecue – hence its iconic red colour. This is a classic, fail-safe Indian dish. Tayvanie always asks for tandoori chicken to be on the menu whenever we have friends at home for dinner.

LAMB CATLESS

Preparation time: 30 minutes
Cooking time: 30 minutes

Serves 6

450g minced lamb
2tsp crushed garlic
1tsp salt
1tsp garam masala
1 chopped green chilli
4 bunches chopped coriander leaves
1 finely chopped onion
2 beaten eggs (to coat)
Breadcrumbs to coat the cutlets
5tbs vegetable oil for frying

* Put the minced lamb in a food processor with the garlic, salt, garam masala, green chilli, coriander leaves and onion.
* Make lemon-sized, flat, oval-shaped patties out of the mixture and coat in the breadcrumbs.
* Dip them in the eggs.
* Shallow fry in vegetable oil until golden brown.

Rashid makes this dish as part of a big feast for Eid al-Fitr, the festival that marks the end of the holy month of Ramadan. Serve these spicy lamb patties hot or cold with my cucumber and mango salad.

FISH TIKKA

Preparation time: 30 minutes
Cooking time: 30 minutes

Serves 8

3tbs olive oil
1 large, chopped onion
1tbs garlic
½tbs dried chillies
4tbs plain or coconut yoghurt
1tbs lemon juice
1tbs tandoori powder
1tbs haldi powder (turmeric)
½tbs garam masala
½tbs salt
800g cubed haddock fillets

* Put all the ingredients, except the fish, into a large bowl and make into a paste.
* Season the fish cubes with the paste.
* Thread fish onto bamboo sticks (or metal skewers) and cook on a low grill for 8 minutes. Allow to cook on both sides.
* Can be served hot or cold.

My schoolfriend, Dhana, moved from Mauritius to India before settling in Manchester in the seventies. She taught me how to make this dish when she came to visit for long weekends. Now, it's one of my staple starters.

FISH VINDAYE

Preparation time: 60 minutes
Cooking time: 30 minutes

Serves 4

100g white fish, e.g. cod or
halibut cut into 2cm chunks.
25ml olive oil
3tbs haldi powder (turmeric)
½tbs garam masala
Salt and pepper
2 sliced large onions
1tbs garlic paste
4tbs mustard seeds
3 whole green chillies – sliced
down the middle
½tsp red chillies
½ lemon

* Season the fish with ¼tsp of the haldi, ¼tsp of the garam masala and a pinch of salt and pepper.
* Heat 15ml of the olive oil.
* Fry the fish, then allow to cool on a plate lined with kitchen roll.
* Gently fry the onion in a pan with the remaining 10ml of oil for 5 minutes.
* When the onion has softened, add the remaining haldi and garam masala. Mix in the garlic paste, mustard seeds and green chillies.
* Add the fried fish chunks and the red chillies. Mix well.
* Remove from the heat and transfer to a bowl. Squeeze the lemon over the fish and allow to cool.

Mauritians always serve this traditional, bright yellow spicy pickle at parties as a pre-dinner nibble. If you have any left over, wrap it in roti for a delicious snack.

HALIM (BROTH)

Preparation time: 60 minutes
Cooking time: 90 minutes

Serves 10

For the halim mix
1tbs coriander powder
1tbs garam masala
5tbs pearl barley
5tbs black lentils
5tbs red lentils
½tbs salt

800g lamb on the bone, cubed –
the leaner the better
3tbs olive oil
2 cubed large onions
800 ml water

To garnish
Chopped coriander leaves
Lemon wedges
Salt

Tip: Use a pressure cooker if you have one to make it extra tender. If not, a normal large pan will also work well.

* Season the lamb with the halim mix and set aside.
* Heat 1tbs oil and fry the onions until golden. Remove and set aside in a bowl.
* Heat 2tbs oil in the large pan. Add the lamb and halim mix and gently fry for 5-10 minutes.
* Add the water. If using a pressure cooker, now transfer and cook for 30 minutes or 1 hour in the pan over a medium heat. Add the onions.
* Add salt to taste and garnish with coriander and lemon wedges.

This hearty, healthy broth was inspired by Rashid, who is a Mauritian Muslim. I cook a big pot of it every fortnight for my nephew, David, to power him through his night shifts as a doctor. And this was always the first thing I'd make for my children when they were ill. Serve with a chapati or baguette.

MEAT

CHICKEN KALIA

Preparation time: 40 minutes. Day-before preparation required.
Cooking time: 50 minutes

Serves 6

6 large potatoes, peeled and
halved
½tsp saffron threads
600g chicken breast, diced into
cubes
3tbs olive oil
2 large, sliced onions

For the marinade
4 large onions
5 crushed garlic cloves
3tbs crushed ginger
½ bunch chopped coriander
½ bunch chopped mint leaves
160g plain or coconut yoghurt
4tbs garam masala
4tbs jeera powder (ground
cumin)
3 cardamom pods
1 large cinnamon stick
2 whole green chillies

* Pierce the potatoes and soak in water with the saffron threads overnight in the fridge.
* To make the marinade, liquidise the onion, garlic and ginger with the coriander and mint. Add the yoghurt, garam masala, jeera, cardamom, cinnamon and green chillies.
* Put all the marinade ingredients in an airtight container and add the chicken. Mix well and allow to marinate overnight.
* Heat the oil. Remove the potatoes from the saffron water, drain well and fry until golden brown.
* Fry the sliced onions until golden brown. Keeping the oil, remove onions from pan and place on a plate lined with kitchen roll to remove excess oil.
* Put the marinated chicken in a pan. Add 2tbs of the oil used for frying the onions. Cook on the hob for 30 minutes on a medium heat. Then add the potatoes and cook for a further 15 minutes. Add the fried onions.
* Garnish with coriander leaves and serve.

Chicken kalia is a popular Mauritian dish and a dinner-party classic.
Prepared with yoghurt, it's lighter than a curry but still has a lovely kick to it.

CHICKEN CURRY

Preparation time: 45 minutes
Cooking time: 60 minutes

Serves 6

1.5kg chicken breast cut into 8 pieces
½tbs garam masala
½tbs jeera powder (ground cumin)
½tbs coriander powder
1tbs crushed ginger
1tbs crushed garlic
10 curry leaves
3tbs olive oil
3 chopped onions
5tbs curry powder (mild or hot according to taste)
1tsp salt
½ bunch chopped coriander leaves
4 fresh tomatoes
275ml water

* Season the chicken with the garam masala, jeera, coriander, half the ginger and garlic and 5 of the curry leaves.
* Heat the oil. Add the onions, curry powder and salt. Stir well.
* Add the remaining 5 curry leaves, half of the chopped coriander leaves and keep stirring. Add the tomatoes and the remaining garlic and ginger.
* Once it becomes a thick sauce, add the seasoned chicken.
* Allow to cook for 30 minutes on a medium heat, then add the water and stir well.
* Simmer for 10 minutes until cooked.
* Garnish with the remaining coriander leaves and serve.

Hands down, this is my favourite dish. Whether it's for a small dinner party or a crowd at a local charity fundraiser, I cook this chicken curry every week. It's easy to make but really rich in flavour. This is Tayvanie and Krishnan's favourite dish.

LAMB CURRY

Preparation time: 60 minutes. Day-before preparation required.
Cooking time: 90 minsminutes

Serves 6

600g boneless lamb, cubed with
fat removed
2tbs garam masala
1tbs crushed ginger
1tbs crushed garlic
¼tsp black pepper
1tsp coriander powder
¼tsp salt
4tbs olive oil
3 chopped onions
4tbs curry powder (mild or hot
according to taste)
4 fresh chopped tomatoes
5 curry leaves
½ bunch fresh coriander
275ml water

*   Marinate the meat with garam masala, ginger, garlic, black pepper, coriander and salt.
*   Allow to marinate overnight or for a minimum of 5 hours. This will make the meat tender and tasty.
*   Heat the oil and fry the onions until golden brown. Add the curry powder and stir for 5 minutes. Then add the chopped tomatoes and curry leaves.
*   Add the meat and half of the water and allow to cook for 20 minutes.
*   Add the rest of the water and allow to cook for a further 10 minutes.
*   Garnish with fresh coriander leaves and serve.

My husband doesn't eat pork or poultry, and my children don't eat beef, so this lamb curry is my go-to dish for a family meal. Delicious and tender, it disappears in minutes!

LAMB AND MUSHROOM

Preparation time: 20 minutes
Cooking time: 45 minutes

Serves 4

400g boneless lamb, sliced
500g washed mushrooms
3 sprigs of mint leaves
½ bunch garlic leaves or spring onions
2½tbs olive oil
½ large coarsely chopped onion
2½tbs dark soy sauce
½tsp cornflour

For the marinade
½tbs fresh garlic crushed or liquidised
½tbs fresh ginger crushed or liquidised
½tsp salt
¼tsp black pepper
½ small finely chopped onion

* Mix the lamb with garlic, ginger, salt, pepper and finely chopped onion. Leave to marinate for 1 hour.
* Meanwhile, slice the mushrooms, chop the mint and cut the garlic leaves or spring onions to 2-3cm in length.
* Heat the oil for about 10 minutes and fry the coarsely chopped onion until golden.
* Add the meat, soy sauce and mushrooms. Keep stirring.
* Mix the cornflour with 1tbs of cold water and add to the pan.
* Add the garlic leaves or spring onions and mint.
* Serve with plain boiled rice and cucumber and carrot salad (p. 76).

A popular Mauritian Creole main course, this dish brings back memories of my mother. A mild alternative to a curry, she'd make it as a treat for birthdays and family celebrations.

LAMB BIRYANI

Preparation time: 60 minutes. Day-before preparation required.
Cooking time: 2 hours120 minutes

Serves 5

1.5kg boneless lamb cut into 6
pieces
5 large white potatoes, peeled
and cut into chunks
1tbs saffron – soaked in 10ml of
freshly boiled water
Salt for seasoning
4 white medium sized onions – 2
to slice and fry, 2 to liquidise for
the marinade
1 bunch fresh coriander leaves
½ bunch fresh mint leaves

For the rice
6 cups basmati rice
4 cinnamon sticks (each about 2
inches long)
6 cardamom pods
½tbs black pepper

For the marinade
260ml plain yoghurt
3tbs fresh crushed garlic
3tbs fresh crushed ginger
3tbs ground coriander
2tbs ground cumin

* In a large, generously greased, hob-proof and oven-proof pot, add all the marinade ingredients and mix well. Wash the lamb, add to the marinade and leave in the fridge overnight or for at least 6 hours.
* Pierce the peeled and cut potatoes then place in a bowl and cover with water. Add the cup of saffron in freshly boiled water and a sprinkle of salt, and leave to soak for one hour, making sure all the potatoes are fully coloured with the saffron.
* Remove the potatoes, keeping the saffron water, and deep fry in the oil and ghee for five minutes until golden brown. Remove and place in a bowl, keeping the oil and ghee.
* Fry the sliced onions until golden brown and caramelised.
* Cover the marinated meat with the potatoes and 1tbs of the onions
* Add 1tsp of the saffron water, 1½tbs of the oil and ghee to the lamb and potato mixture and place the pot on a medium heat for 10 minutes until it is bubbling.
* Wash and drain the rice.
* Boil 300ml of water with cinnamon sticks and cardamon pods. When the water is boiling add the rice and continue boiling for 3 minutes. Drain well.
* Carefully spoon the rice onto the top of the lamb and potato mixture. Add the caramelised fried onions, then sprinkle the chopped coriander and mint on the top.
* Sprinkle 3tbs of the saffron water and then 5tbs

4 cinnamon sticks about 2 inches long
6 cardamon pods
3 whole green chillies

For frying
300ml vegetable oil
5tbs ghee

of the oil and ghee onto the rice in a circular fashion around the pot.

* Cover the pot with foil, making sure it is well sealed around the edges, then cover with its lid and place in 180C pre-heated oven for 1 hour. Reduce the heat to 100C for another 1 hour.

* To check it's cooked, remove the foil, taking care of the steam. Insert a bamboo skewer into the pot, if there is no resistance, it is cooked.

* Once cooked and ready to serve, separate the rice from the meat and potato and put into a separate bowl. Don't worry too much if some rice remains with the meat mixture.

* Place the meat and potatoes mixture – sometimes called the masala of the biryani –in another serving dish. When serving, place some from each dish onto the plate.

FISH

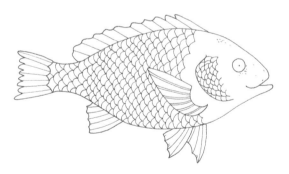

LOBSTER MADRAS WITH COCONUT MILK

Preparation time: 60 minutes
Cooking time: 45 minutes

Serves 6

3 lobster tails
1tbs crushed garlic
1tbs crushed ginger
1tsp salt
1tsp black pepper
1tsp ground cumin
3tbs vegetable oil
2 sliced onions
6 curry leaves
4tbs madras curry powder (mild
or hot according to taste)
2 chopped tomatoes
6tbs coconut milk
1 bunch coriander leaves

* Prepare the lobster: Dip it in boiling water. Remove from the shell and season with half the garlic and ginger. Add the salt, pepper and cumin.
* Heat the oil on a medium heat. Add the onion, curry leaves and curry powder. Keep stirring for 5 minutes.
* Add the chopped tomatoes and the rest of the ginger and garlic. Cook for 15 minutes.
* Add the lobster and cook for a further 5 minutes.
* Add the coconut milk. Allow to cook for 5 minutes.
* Sprinkle with coriander leaves before serving.

I first tried lobster madras at a family-run Indian restaurant in Marylebone. I was so impressed that I decided to experiment at home with my own version. A real wow-factor dish – save this one for special occasions. Krishnan asks me to cook it each year for his birthday.

STUFFED RED SNAPPERS

Preparation time: 60 minutes
Cooking time: 45 minutes

Serves 4

4 large red snappers (cleaned,
scaled and head removed)
1tbs crushed garlic
1tsp salt
2 pinches saffron soaked in 3tbs
warm water
3tbs olive oil
1 fresh lemon

For the stuffing
5 chestnuts, boiled and mashed
½ sweet potato, boiled and
mashed
1tbs crushed garlic
2tbs garam masala
½tsp ground cardamom
3 sprigs of thyme
3 sprigs of chopped parsley

* Season the fish individually with the garlic, salt,
saffron water and olive oil.
* To make the stuffing, mix the mashed chestnuts and
sweet potato, garlic, garam masala, cardamom, thyme
and parsley into a paste.
* Stuff the fish and allow to marinate for one hour.
Wrap the fish individually in foil and place on an
ovenproof tray.
* Preheat the oven to gas mark 4/170C. Place the tray
in the middle of the oven for 45 minutes.
* Serve garnished with lemon wedges and tomato
chutney (p.83).

*I decided to make stuffed red snappers one Christmas as an alternative to turkey. I added chestnuts
to the recipe for festive flair, and it gave the dish a deliciously sweet and nutty flavour. Make this dish
if you really want to impress your guests.*

SPICY PRAWN AND EGG NOODLES

Preparation time: 30 minutes
Cooking time: 30 minutes

Serves 4

1tbs olive oil
2tbs curry powder (mild or hot
according to taste)
2tbs crushed garlic
300g raw prawns (peeled)
½ thinly cut cabbage
4 eggs
400g egg noodles, fresh or dried
and reconstituted.
1tbs oyster sauce
2tbs dark soy sauce
1 bunch spring onions or garlic
chives leaves

* Heat the oil on a medium heat. Add the curry powder and garlic, followed quickly by the prawns and cabbage.
* While the prawns and cabbage are cooking, make an omelette with the eggs and cut it into small pieces.
* In a large wok, heat a small amount of oil and add the noodles.
* Add the prawns, cabbage and omelette to the noodles and stir fry.
* Add the oyster and soy sauce.
* Sprinkle with finely chopped fresh spring onions and serve with tomato chutney (page 83).

I always keep a packet of egg noodles in my cupboard, so that when friends pop in unexpectedly, I can whip this dish up. Super simple and so tasty. Serve with tomato chutney. Jonathan, my youngest nephew's favourite dish.

SEABASS CURRY

Preparation time: 30 minutes
Cooking time: 20 minutes

Serves 4

4 pieces boneless seabass (any
white fish can be used)
Salt and pepper for seasoning
1tsp garam masala
3tbs olive oil
2 chopped medium onions
3tbs curry powder (mild or hot
according to taste)
1tsp ginger paste
1tsp garlic paste
½ small finely chopped red chilli
(optional for added fire!)
10 ml water
2 curry leaves (washed)
2tbs fresh coriander, washed and
chopped
2 fresh chopped tomatoes
¼tsp tamarind sauce – seeds
remove

* Season the fish with salt and pepper and ½tsp garam masala and gently fry, being careful not to overcook.
* To make the curry sauce, heat the oil on a medium heat and fry the onion. Add the curry powder, ginger, garlic, red chilli and 10ml of water.
* Mix in the curry leaves, half the coriander and the remaining garam masala. Keep stirring and add the chopped tomatoes.
* Mix the tamarind with 1tbs of water and add to the sauce.
* Put the fish in the curry sauce and cook for about 10 minutes.
* Transfer into a serving dish and garnish with the leftover coriander.

In Mauritius, we always had seabass curry at Easter. My father would go down to the port early in the morning to pick up fresh fish, and my mother would make a big curry for all our family and friends.

FISH CURRY WITH AUBERGINE

Preparation time: 60 minutes
Cooking time: 45 minutes

Serves 6

8 steaks of cod/halibut
10tbs olive oil
1 onion chopped into small cubes
5 curry leaves
6tbs curry powder (mild or hot according to taste)
1tbs minced garlic and ginger
1tsp salt
3 chopped fresh tomatoes
1 small, chopped chilli
¼tbs tamarind water
4 medium sliced aubergines
½ bunch fresh coriander
Extra oil for frying the fish

For the marinade
1tsp salt
1tsp garam masala
¼tsp jeera powder (ground cumin)

* Marinate the fish with salt, garam masala and jeera for 1 hour.
* Gently fry the fish in 7tbs olive oil until golden brown. Do not overcook.
* In another pan, use 3tbs olive oil to fry the onions, curry leaves, curry powder, garlic and ginger and 1tsp salt. Stir well for a few minutes.
* Add the chopped tomatoes, chilli and tamarind water. Allow to cook for 10 minutes, then gently simmer for a further 10 minutes.
* Add the aubergine and fried fish and allow to cook for a further 15 minutes.
* Plate and garnish with fresh coriander leaves.

The traditional fish and aubergine curry, or cari poisson, is hugely popular in Mauritius. Use fish steaks or fillets, to avoid bones, and serve with chutneys, salad and chapatis or rice and pickles.

VEGETARIAN

SAVOY CABBAGE WITH COCONUT, TURMERIC AND DRIED RED CHILLIES

Preparation time: 30 minutes
Cooking time: 30 minutes

Serves 4

1½tbs olive oil
2 chopped onions
2tbs turmeric
1tbs mustard seeds
1tbs crushed red chillies
1 finely chopped savoy cabbage,
washed and dried
½tsp salt
1tbs grated coconut
4 curry leaves
½ bunch coriander

* Heat the oil on a medium heat and fry the onions. Add the turmeric, mustard seeds and crushed red chillies and blend together. Add the cabbage.
* Keep stirring and add the salt, grated coconut and curry leaves.
* Drain any excess oil. Garnish with fresh coriander leaves and serve.

This spicy cabbage stir-fry works brilliantly as a side dish to any main meal. Healthy and simple, I always use a tablespoon of coconut to add sweetness.

BROWN LENTILS

Preparation time: 30 minutes. Day-before preparation required.
Cooking time: 60 minsminutes

Serves 4

150g brown lentils (soak overnight)
1tsp salt
3 chopped basil leaves
600ml lemongrass stock or vegetable stock
3tbs olive oil
½ tinned tomatoes in own juice
2 finely chopped white onions
½tbs crushed garlic
½tbs crushed ginger
3 sprigs of chopped parsley
3 sprigs of thyme
1 sliced white onion

Tip: You can use a pressure cooker to reduce cooking time for the lentils.

*   Boil the lentils for one hour with salt, basil leaves and lemongrass stock/vegetable stock .
*   Heat half the oil on a medium heat and add the tinned tomatoes, finely chopped onion, garlic, ginger, parsley and thyme to make a tomato sauce. Allow to simmer for 10 minutes.
*   Heat the other half of the oil and fry the sliced onions until golden brown.
*   Once the tomato sauce is cooked, add to the lentils.
*   Serve the lentils garnished with the golden fried onions and fresh coriander.

This is such a hearty, filling dish that it can be served as a side or as a main meal. My mother would regularly make spiced lentils for dinner, served with rice and vegetables. The rich, earthy brown lentils and the fragrant lemongrass make a mouth-watering combination.

This dish can alternatively be used with any lentils.

MIXED VEGETABLE CURRY

Preparation time: 60 minutes
Cooking time: 30 minutes

Serves 4

5tbs olive oil
2 chopped onions
5tbs curry powder (mild or hot
according to taste)
1tsp garam masala
3 curry leaves
1tsp ginger paste
1tsp garlic paste
3 medium potatoes cut in quar-
ters and pre-boiled
Mixed chopped vegetables:
carrots, cauliflower, peas, green
beans, broccoli, sweetcorn
2 medium aubergines cut in
2-inch cubes
3 chopped tomatoes
¼ bunch coriander

* Heat the oil on a medium heat and fry the onions in a saucepan. Add the curry powder, garam masala, curry leaves, garlic and ginger paste. Allow the paste to cook while stirring for 10 minutes.
* Add the potatoes, mixed vegetables, aubergine, tomatoes and most of the coriander.
* Add salt to taste.
* Allow to cook for 30 minutes.
* Garnish with the remaining fresh coriander and serve with boiled rice and a fresh green salad.

Packed with vegetables, I'd make this dish every week when my children were growing up – and it's still a firm favourite. I always add sweetcorn for colour.

CABBAGE AND COCONUT STIR FRY

Preparation time: 15 minutes
Cooking time: 10 minutes

Serves 4

3tbs olive oil
1tbs haldi powder (turmeric)
1tbs dry chillies
4 chopped garlic cloves
¼tsp salt
4 curry leaves
2tbs grated coconut (unsweet-
ened)
½ flat cabbage (alternative white
cabbage) washed, dried and
chopped very finely
3 chopped sprigs of coriander

* Heat the oil and add the haldi powder, chillies, garlic, salt, curry leaves and grated coconut.
* Keep stirring. Do not allow to burn.
* Add the cabbage, keep stirring for 10 minutes.
* Drain any excess oil and transfer to a large dish.
* Serve garnished with fresh chopped coriander.

This dish is ideal for vegetarians. Serve with rice or naan bread.

CHOU CHOU (CHRISTOPHINE) WITH FRESH CHILLIES

Preparation time: 30 minutes
Cooking time: 30 minutes

Serves 4

2tbs olive oil
2 chopped onions
4 chou chous (or one medium-sized marrow), peeled and chopped in wedges
¼tsp salt
2 chopped tomatoes
3 fresh chillies, halved
¼ bunch parsley (fresh or dry)
¼ bunch thyme (fresh or dry)

* Heat the oil on a medium heat and fry the onions for a few minutes then add the chou chou.
* Add the salt, tomatoes, chillies, parsley and thyme.
* Allow to cook for 30 minutes.
* Garnish with a sprig of fresh thyme or coriander leaves.

The chou chou – also known as chayote or christophine – is from the same family as melon, cucumber and squash and is a common Mauritian vegetable – most families have a chou chou vine growing in the garden. You can serve it in curries, have it raw or pickle it – but my favourite way to eat it is sautéed with chillies. An alternative for chou chou is a medium-sized marrow.

CAULIFLOWER / JEERA CURRY

Preparation time: 30 minutes
Cooking time: 30 minutes

Serves 6

2tbs olive oil
2 sliced medium onions
2tbs curry powder (mild or hot
according to taste)
¼tsp salt
½tbs jeera powder (ground
cumin)
5 curry leaves
½tsp ground ginger and garlic
2 fresh green chillies
3 chopped tomatoes
1 large cauliflower, washed and
separated into florets
2tbs water
½ bunch coriander

* Heat the oil on a medium heat and fry the onions. Add the curry powder, salt, jeera, curry leaves, ginger and garlic, chillies and chopped tomatoes. The sauce should have a paste-like texture.
* Add the cauliflower, water and most of the coriander leaves.
* Allow to cook for 30 minutes.
* Garnish with the remaining coriander leaves.

In my view, cauliflower tastes best crunchy and spicy. I serve this dish as an accompaniment to fish curry, or I make it without the chillies for my one-year-old grandson, Ashwin.

Jeera is also known as cumin.

PUMPKIN WITH DRIED RED CHILLIES, SHREDDED COCONUT AND MUSTARD SEEDS

Preparation time: 30 minutes
Cooking time: 40 minutes

Serves 6

3tsp olive oil
2 chopped onions
5 curry leaves
1tsp garlic and ginger paste
500g pumpkin, peeled and
chopped into small pieces
½tsp salt
¼tsp dried red chillies
1tsp shredded coconut
2 chopped tomatoes
½tsp mustard seeds
¼ bunch fresh coriander

* Heat the oil on a medium heat and fry the onions. Add the curry leaves, garlic and ginger paste, and fry.
* Add the pumpkin, salt, chillies, shredded coconut, tomatoes, mustard seeds and coriander leaves.
* Allow to cook for 30 minutes or until the pumpkin is soft.
* Garnish with fresh coriander leaves.

During Hindu festivals, there's no form of meat, poultry, eggs or seafood. Instead, tables are laden with flatbreads, platters of aromatic basmati rice and a whole array of vegetable dishes – and pumpkin is nearly always on the menu. Mild and flavoursome, I cooked this dish for my son-in-law, Adam, to introduce him to Mauritian cuisine. He never looked back.

SPINACH AND DAL CURRY

Preparation time: 15 minutes. Day-before preparation required.
Cooking time: 15 minsminutes

Serves 6

160g chana dal
200ml water
1tsp salt
10g garlic and ginger paste
1tsp jeera powder (ground cumin)
5 curry leaves
2 chopped onions
¼tsp curry powder (mild or hot according to taste)
½tsp garam masala
1tsp dried chillies
¼ bunch fresh coriander
3 chopped tomatoes
300g baby spinach, washed
¼tsp mustard seeds

* Soak the chana dal for 5 hours or overnight.
* Boil the chana dal in the 200ml water for 30 minutes with salt, garlic and ginger paste, jeera and 2 curry leaves.
* To make the curry sauce, heat oil in a saucepan, fry the onion, add the curry powder, garam masala, dried chillies, remaining curry leaves and a few coriander leaves.
* Keep stirring and add the chopped tomatoes and salt to taste.
* Add the curry sauce to the pot of chana dal. Allow to cook for 10 minutes.
* Add the spinach and mustard seeds. Allow to cook for a further 5 minutes.
* Garnish with fresh coriander leaves and serve with cucumber and carrot salad (p. 76).

You'll usually find spinach and dal curry in an Indian thali – a variety of complementing dishes on a single plate. Most of the women in our family suffer from anaemia, so this dish is also a delicious way of boosting our iron intake!

AUBERGINE WITH TOMATO SAUCE

Preparation time: 30 minutes
Cooking time: 30 minutes

Serves 4

3 thinly sliced long aubergines
1tsp salt
3tbs olive oil
2 chopped onions
3 curry leaves
4 chopped tomatoes
3 medium green chillies
¼ bunch fresh coriander

* Slice the aubergines and salt lightly. After 15 minutes, condensation should appear on the surface of the sliced aubergine. Remove the water with a kitchen towel. Salting the aubergine withdraws the water and any bitterness and allows the texture to be preserved after cooking.
* Fry the aubergine and put to one side.
* Heat oil on a medium heat and fry the onions till golden brown.
* Add the curry leaves and fry for a minute before adding the tomatoes, green chillies and a little water. Cook for 20 minutes on a gentle heat.
* Add the fried aubergines and coriander leaves and allow to cook for 10 minutes.
* Transfer to a dish, garnish with fresh coriander leaves and serve with boiled rice.

Aubergine – or eggplant or brinzel – is a popular vegetable in Mauritius. Tomatoes are also used in many of our dishes, so the two are often combined for mouth-watering meals.
Perfect for vegetarians.

SAUTÉED CAULIFLOWER

Preparation time: 20 minutes
Cooking time: 15 minutes

Serves 4

2tbs olive oil
2 large onions
4 curry leaves
1tbs mustard seeds
½tbs ground garlic
½tbs ground ginger
1 medium sized chopped chilli
1 medium sized cauliflow-
er, washed, dried and finely
chopped
¼ bunch of fresh coriander

* Heat the oil and fry the onions until golden brown, and add the curry leaves, mustard seeds, garlic, ginger and chilli.
* Keep stirring.
* Add the cauliflower and stir until golden brown.
* Add salt to taste.
* Garnish with fresh chopped coriander leaves.

This dish is ideal to serve with boiled rice and dal. Tayvanie's favourite dish – she will eat it with roti instead of rice.

SIDES

CUCUMBER AND CARROT SALAD

Preparation time: 15 minutes

Serves 6

½tbs extra virgin olive oil
¼tsp salt
¼tsp white pepper
1 large onion, sliced
¼tsp vinegar
1 cucumber, peeled and grated
2 large carrots, peeled and
grated

* Mix the extra virgin olive oil, salt, pepper, sliced onion and vinegar.
* Add the cucumber and carrots.
* Keep refrigerated until time to serve.

Healthy and tasty, this carrot and cucumber salad is easy to make and the perfect sidekick to an Indian biryani.

CUCUMBER AND MANGO SALAD

Preparation time: 30 minutes

Serves 6

1 large thinly sliced onion
¼tsp white pepper
¼tsp salt
¼tsp vinegar
1tsp extra virgin olive oil
1 large cucumber, peeled and
sliced
1 large ripe mango, peeled and
sliced

* Mix the sliced onion with white pepper, salt, vinegar and extra virgin olive oil.
* Add the cucumber and mango.
* Keep refrigerated until time to serve.

We had three mango trees in our back garden in Mauritius. My sister and I would pick the fruit, slice it up and eat it fresh, juice running down our faces and arms. This refreshing salad works well with my tandoori chicken or lamb catlass.

CHAPATIS

Preparation time: 20 minutes
Cooking time: 10 minutes

Makes 6

150g chapati flour
Pinch of salt
110ml cold water

Tip: Place baking paper between the cooked chapatis so they don't stick together.

* Sift flour and salt into a bowl.
* Make a well in the centre and add a small amount of the water then hand-mix, adding water until the dough is slightly sticky.
* Knead for 10 minutes.
* Place in a bowl, cover with a damp tea towel and leave in a warm area for 30 minutes, allowing the dough to rise.
* Divide into 6 equal portions then roll into balls.
* On a floured worktop, roll into thin circles, approx. 15cm in diameter.
* Heat a flat, non-stick frying pan and cook the dough circles, one at a time, 30 seconds each side.
* Place the cooked chapatis on a plate, separated with baking paper, and loosely cover with a tea towel/kitchen towel to keep warm and dry.

You can buy chapatis pre-made, but nothing quite beats the welcoming smell and satisfaction of serving your own warm, freshly made stack. Needing just a few ingredients, they're easier to make than you think.

NAAN BREAD

Preparation time: 30 minutes
Cooking time: 30 minutes

Serves 8

¾ cup of warm water
3tsp instant yeast
½tbs sugar
300g plain flour
4tbs olive oil
½ cup of low fat live plain yogurt
2 eggs
¾tsp salt

For topping
3tsp melted butter
1tbs minced garlic
3 chopped sprigs of coriander leaves

* In a jug, combine the warm water, yeast and sugar and allow to rise for 20 minutes.
* Sieve the flour into a large bowl and make a hole in the middle.
* Add the risen yeast to the flour, followed by the olive oil, yogurt, eggs and salt. Mix until it forms a sticky dough.
* Knead the dough until smooth.
* Place the dough in a greased bowl and allow it to rise for 2 hours. You will notice the dough double in size.
* Divide the dough into 8 balls.
* In a flat pan, heat a small amount of oil.
* Roll the ball on a floured flat surface. Do not use too much flour.
* Put the flat dough on the pan for 3 minutes and turn over for another 2 minutes until golden brown.
* Remove from the pan and brush with the melted butter, garlic and chopped coriander leaves.
* Place in a dish and cover with a tea towel/kitchen towel to keep warm. Continue until you have used the 8 balls of dough.

TOMATO CHUTNEY

Preparation time: 30 minutes

Serves 6

5 tomatoes (slightly unripe)
2 finely chopped red onions
½ finely chopped small chilli
¼ bunch finely chopped coriander
Pinch of salt

* Remove the seeds from the tomatoes. Cut into small cubes.
* Mix with the onions, chopped chilli and coriander leaves.
* Keep refrigerated in an air-tight container. Add salt to taste just before serving.

Tomato chutney is one of my best-loved accompaniments, complementing snacks, fritters, noodles, biryani and many other dishes.

SAFFRON RICE

Preparation time: 5 minutes
Cooking time: 10 minutes

Serves 4

225g basmati rice
370ml water
4 cardamom pods
½tsp jeera powder (ground
cumin)
½tsp garam masala
¼tsp saffron threads soaked in
1tbs warm water
Pinch of salt
1tbs fried onions

* Soak the rice in cold water for 30 minutes to get the grains fluffy then rinse.
* Boil the water for 10 minutes with a pinch of salt, the cardamom pods, jeera powder and garam masala. Add the soaked rice and cover with a tight lid.
* Allow to cook for 8 minutes.
* Once the rice is cooked, turn off the heat and remove the lid, allowing the steam to evaporate.
* Sprinkle the saffron around the pan and use a fork to blend it as you fluff up the rice. Put the fried onions on top and cover with the lid.
* Serve hot.

I usually make plain basmati rice, but on special occasions, out comes the saffron rice! Saffron adds such a lovely, bright golden colour to the rice, contrasting with the crimson saffron threads. I add fried onions for extra flavour.

GREEN BANANAS

Preparation time: 30 minutes
Cooking time: 30 minutes

Serves 8

6 large green bananas
¼tsp salt
¼tsp jeera powder (ground cumin)
5tbs olive oil
1 small, chopped onion
2tbs curry powder (mild or hot according to taste)
1tsp crushed garlic
1tsp crushed ginger
4 curry leaves
1tbs mustard seeds
2 chopped green chillies
¼tsp tamarind paste
¼ bunch chopped fresh coriander

*   Boil the bananas in their skins for 10 minutes until hard and the skin becomes black. Add the salt and jeera and allow to cool.
*   Remove the skin and grate the bananas.
*   Coat the bananas with 1tbs of the olive oil to prevent them from becoming sticky.
*   Heat the remaining oil and fry the onion.
*   Add the curry powder, garlic, ginger, curry leaves, mustard seeds, chopped chillies and tamarind paste. Cook for 30 minutes.
*   Add the bananas.
*   Garnish with fresh coriander.

Green bananas are abundant in Mauritius. Firmer than yellow bananas and with a distinct bitter taste, they are a cheap food source and a good starchy ingredient for savoury dishes. On Fridays, my mother would make a mix of vegetarian dishes for dinner – and green banana curry was usually one of them.

TURMERIC

CORIANDER POWDER

curry powder

Saffron

Ghee

TANDOORI MASALA

SPICE BLEND

GARAM MASALA

MUSTARD SEEDS

SPICES CUPBOARD

SPICES CUPBOARD

All the spices in my recipes are available in Indian supermarkets and most high-street grocery stores. It's best to use fresh spices and to keep them for no more than one year (or as stated on the packet). Trust your sense of smell!

Keep spices in an airtight container, label with the date that you opened them, and store in a cool, dark cupboard or the fridge if required.

When toasting spices, use a heavy, cast-iron pan over a medium heat and continuously stir. Avoid overcooking spices – once the aroma is released, they are cooked, any longer and they can become bitter. Allow to fully cool before grinding them.

CARDAMOM PODS

Used widely in Indian cuisine, cardamom pods are used to add a nutty flavour. It tastes better when you add the pod whole as the juice comes out when cooked. The green cardamom pods tend to have a stronger aroma.

CHILLIES

If you have any leftover chillies, it's a good idea to dry them on a piece of kitchen roll at room temperature for twenty-four hours and then grind for future use.

CINNAMON

You can use cinnamon sticks or ground cinnamon in both sweet and savoury dishes. If you choose sticks, remember to take them out of the dish before serving, as you cannot eat them.

CORIANDER LEAVES

Often used as a garnish, coriander leaves should be green, with no hint of yellow, and have a strong aroma. Always buy fresh and keep refrigerated.

CORIANDER SEEDS AND CORIANDER POWDER

The seeds are from the flowers of the coriander plant. You get a nutty aroma when toasted and ground. Coriander seeds don't burn quickly and can be toasted on a high heat.

CUMIN SEEDS (JEERA)

Jeera is spelled in various ways across different Asian countries, so be mindful when shopping. The seeds have a very nutty and earthy flavour with a strong aroma.

CURRY POWDER

Curry powder is a mix of spices – usually turmeric, chilli powder, ground coriander, ground jeera, ground ginger and pepper. Always keep a jar in your cupboard.

GARAM MASALA MIX

Garam masala is another special mix of spices which differs from curry powder. Make your own by putting 5tsp fennel seeds, 5 curry leaves, 1tsp jeera, 1tsp cloves, 3tsp cinnamon powder, 3tsp black ground peppercorns and 3tbs coriander seeds in a non-stick pan and toast for 5 minutes while stirring. Allow to cool and then grind.

CURRY LEAVES

Curry leaves can be tricky to find, so stock up, grind and store. Remove the leaves from the stalks before using.

GARLIC AND GINGER PASTE

Peel 250g fresh root ginger and 10 garlic bulbs. Blend into a paste in a food blender. This is best when fresh.

LEMONGRASS STOCK

To make lemongrass stock, you need:
½tbs olive oil
2 large chopped onions
3tbs fresh ginger
2 ground curry leaves
½tsp garam masala
½tsp salt
½tsp black pepper
570ml water
6 stalks of lemongrass

Heat the oil, add the onion and fry until light brown. Add the ginger, curry leaves, garam masala, salt and pepper, and stir for five minutes. Add the water and the lemongrass stalks, and simmer for one hour. Allow to cool then liquidise the stock. Keep refrigerated or freeze. This stock is sufficient for a dish for six people.

GHEE

The Indian version of clarified butter, used for frying.

HALDI POWDER (TURMERIC)

In the UK, you can get dried turmeric rhizomes in most supermarkets. Peel and finely cube five fresh rhizomes. Dry out in the sun for two days and then grind. Allow to dry out again in the sun for two days before storing in an airtight jar.

MUSTARD SEEDS

These small, round, dried seeds of the mustard plant release a nutty flavour when fried.

PAPRIKA

The ground, bright red powder from sweet and hot dried peppers, paprika adds a beautiful colour to food but without the fieriness of chilli powder.

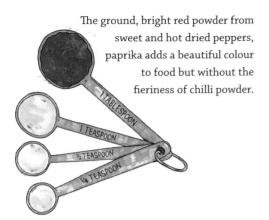

SAFFRON (ZAFRAN)

Derived from the flower of a crocus, saffron is said to be more expensive than gold because harvesting it is so laborious. Beware of cheap imitations, which are usually adulterated by being padded out. Iran and Spain are two of the main producers of good quality saffron.

TAMARIND PASTE

The tamarind tree produces pod-like fruit which contains a sharp-tasting, edible pulp. To dilute, take a tablespoon of the paste and add 2tbs warm water.

SOYA SAUCE

TANDOORI MASALA

Tandoori masala is a marinade used to flavour meat and fish. Make your own by blending:

3tbs ground coriander
1tbs jeera
1tbs ground cumin
1tbs garlic paste
1tbs ginger paste
1tsp cloves
1tbs paprika
1tsp salt
1tbs haldi powder

THYME

This aromatic herb is used in fricassee recipes (classic French stews) and certain dishes with tomatoes and garlic, such as rougaille.

INDEX

A.
Aubergine:
* Aubergine Fritters 14
* Aubergine with Tomato Sauce 70
* Fish Curry with Aubergine 50

B.
Bread:
* Chapatis 79
* Naan Bread 80

Broth 26
Brown Lentils 56

C.
Cabbage and Coconut Stir Fry 61

Cauliflower:
* Cauliflower / Jeera Curry 64
* Sautéed Cauliflower 72

Chapatis 87

Chicken:
* Chicken Curry 32
* Chicken Kalia 30
* Tandoori Chicken 18

Chilli:
* Chilli Cakes and Coconut Sambal 12
* Chou Chou (Christophine) with Fresh Chillies 62
* Pumpkin with Dried Red Chillies, Shredded Coconut and Mustard Seeds 67
* Savoy Cabbage with Coconut, Turmeric And Dried Red Chillies 54

Chou Chou (Christophine) with Fresh Chillies 62

Coconut:
* Cabbage and Coconut Stir Fry 61
* Chilli Cakes and Coconut Sambal 12
* Lobster Madras with Coconut Milk 42
* Pumpkin with Dried Red Chillies, Shredded Coconut and Mustard Seeds 67
* Savoy Cabbage with Coconut, Turmeric and Dried Red Chillies 54

Cucumber:
* Cucumber and Carrot Salad 76
* Cucumber and Mango Salad 78

Curry:
* Cauliflower / Jeera Curry 64
* Chicken Curry 32
* Fish Curry with Aubergine 50
* Lamb Curry 34
* Mixed Vegetable Curry 59
* Seabass Curry 48
* Spinach and Dal Curry 69

F.
Fish:
* Fish Curry with Aubergine 50
* Fish Samosas 9
* Fish Tikka 23
* Fish Vindaye 25
* Lobster Madras with Coconut Milk 42

* Seabass Curry 48
* Spicy Prawn and Egg Noodles 47
* Stuffed Red Snappers 44

H.
Halim 26

G.
Green Bananas 86

L.
Lamb:
* Lamb and Mushroom 37
* Lamb Biryani 38
* Lamb Catless 20
* Lamb Curry 34
* Mutton or Lamb Rolls 4

Lobster Madras with Coconut Milk 42

M.
Mixed Vegetable Curry 59
Mutton or Lamb Rolls 4

N.
Naan Bread 80

O.
Onion Bhajas (Bhaji) 6

P.
Pumpkin with Dried Red Chillies, Shredded

Coconut and Mustard Seeds 67

S.
Saffron Rice 85
Sautéed Cauliflower 72
Savoy Cabbage with Coconut, Turmeric and Dried Red Chillies 54
Seabass Curry 48
Spices Cupboard 89
Spicy Prawn and Egg Noodles 47
Spinach and Dal Curry 69
Stuffed Red Snappers 44

T.
Tandoori Chicken 18
Tomato Chutney 83

ACKNOWLEDGEMENTS

Thank you to my mother for the wonderful Mauritian food I grew up with, my father for encouraging me to dream big and my grandfather for educating me, at such an early age, about herbs and spices, their smells, tastes and uses.

I thank my two children, Tayvanie and Krishnan, who have been my fiercest food critics and biggest fans over the years. And my husband, Rashid, for his endless support.

A big thanks to my sister, Jo, my brother-in-law, Mario, and their two boys, David and Jonathan, who have appreciated my cooking for so many years.

To my friends, Prabha Chinien, Dhana Underwood, Corinne Decupère and Shirley Achaibar who encouraged me to write these recipes.

To my son-in-law, Adam Winchester, who never fails to compliment my cooking, and to Clémence Leray for her patience, encouragement and skilful artistic direction in putting this book together.

To Nicola Cawthorn and Nikki Thompson for all their help with my handwritten manuscripts and endless changes.

Thank you to all the tasters and everyone who enjoys these recipes.